Love by the Book

Love by the Book

the Book

WHAT THE SONG OF SOLOMON
SAYS ABOUT SEXUALITY, ROMANCE,
AND THE BEAUTY OF MARRIAGE

WALTER C. KAISER JR.

LEXHAM PRESS

Love by the Book: What the Song of Solomon Says about Sexuality, Romance, and the Beauty of Marriage
© 2016 by Walter C. Kaiser Jr.

Lexham Press, 1313 Commercial St., Bellingham, WA 98225
LexhamPress.com

First edition by Weaver Book Company.

Print ISBN 9781683591801
Digital ISBN 9781683591818

Cover design: Frank Gutbrod
Interior design: Frank Gutbrod
Editorial: Line for Line Publishing Services

For all those beautiful God-honoring marriages

That evidence the love, joy, and deep affection for each other

As God intended for them to enjoy and mirror

for society at large!

CONTENTS

Introducing the Bible's Best Song:

It's on Sexuality, Romantic Love, and the Beauty of Marriage 9

Chapter 1

God's Gift of Romantic Love (1:1–2:17) 23

Love's Desire for an Absent Lover (1:1–4) 34

Love's Feeling of Unworthiness (1:5–7) 36

Love's Comparisons (1:8–17) 37

Love's Virtues (2:1–7) 40

Love's Anticipations (2:8–17) 42

Chapter 2

God's Gift of Intimate Marital Love (3:1–5:8) 49

The Longing for Marital Love (3:1–5) 56

Two Interludes (3:6–11; 4:1–7) 57

The Prospect of Marital Love (4:8–11) 61

The Exclusiveness of Marital Love (4:12–15) 62

The Privacy of Marital Love (4:16–5:1) 64

The Jealousy of Marital Love (5:2–5:8) 65

Chapter 3

God's Gift of Abiding Love (5:9–8:14) *73*

In Praise of the Shepherd-Boyfriend (5:9–6:2) *73*

Our Memory of Love's Courtship (6:3–8:4) *75*

Our Experience of Love's Invincibility (8:5–7) *81*

Our Appreciation of Love's Guardians (8:8–14) *85*

INTRODUCING THE BIBLE'S BEST SONG

IT'S ON SEXUALITY, ROMANTIC LOVE, AND THE BEAUTY OF MARRIAGE

*S*ome today humorously say, "Read or study the Song of Solomon? I'm too young to do that!"

But that remark is as old as what some of the early church fathers such as Origen and Jerome intoned: a person should not read the Song of Solomon until reaching 30 years of age. At the close of the nineteenth century, Rev. E. P. Eddrupp, prebendary of Salisbury Cathedral, said that the Song of Solomon may not be fitted for public reading in a mixed congregation, or even for private reading by the impure in heart.

Meanwhile, in the twenty-first century the whole biblical concept of marriage and family is under massive attack. The Bible has been forgotten or deliberately dropped from our everyday usage as an authority on what a godly marriage is and what a properly functioning family unit looks like.

Mention in today's culture the word "marriage" to someone who is between 18 and 29 years of age and you might get a blank stare or a question in return: Why would a person want to get married in these times?

Even all too many married couples who attend evangelical churches have stopped being romantic to one another shortly after their weddings! The word "romantic," many will add, is a secular word and nothing in Scripture calls for us to be affectionate. Thus, many believing couples have dropped arranging dates with each other. If the truth be told, all too many will confess that their marriages are dull, are boring, and involve a relationship where they just take each other for granted. There are few, if any, occasions where they set aside time to adore, admire, and appreciate parts of God's creation as a fun portion of their vacation plans, much less adore, admire, or appreciate each other. Instead of a vibrant joy of sharing in the grace of life with each other, a repetitious tedium has set in over the years and nothing can convince either partner that God never intended their married days to be so unpleasant, redundant, and boring.

How did our culture go from the gross immorality of the 1960s, when Joseph Fletcher said "if the situation presents itself, just do it," to a culture that substitutes same-sex love for love between spouses? Instead of the intimacy between devoted couples, the rule seems to be that one should do whatever feels good in order to fulfill one's sexual needs. Just don't get encumbered with a lifelong marriage is the word on the streets!

In addition, the June 28, 1969, Stonewall riots in New York became the catalyst for the organization of gay rights groups, which argue that it is a civil right for both men and women to have sex with someone of the same gender and with as many partners as they wish. One can observe the moral collapse of an ethically pure culture right before our very eyes. The people of Sodom and Gomorrah will have nothing that will shock us morally, or that our culture has not imitated and championed in our own day. How will a holy God be able to continue to restrain his hand of judgment, unless there comes a revival of his people—one that lives out the teaching of Scripture regarding marriage and family? But our Lord has not left us to our own devices on this topic, for both by his presence at the marriage feast of Cana (John 2) and by his teaching in the book of Song of Solomon, he wants us to be well informed on what he expects in these areas.

HOW DOES THE SONG OF SONGS FIT IN THE BIBLE?

Part of our problem comes from the fact that when we approach the Bible, many of us expect it only has to do with our redemption and salvation in Christ. But the Song of Songs deals extensively with another topic apart from redemption in Christ. If this book had as its purpose to point to Christ, then it has to be interpreted allegorically and symbolically, which is what many have done. In the past, the Christian church sang, and some Christians still do, hymns such as "Jesus, Rose of Sharon," and "The Lily of the Valley," modeled after the metaphors in chapter 2 of the Song of Songs. Yet, did not the apostle Paul say in 2 Timothy 3:16–17 that "all Scripture is profitable for reproof, correction, and training in righteousness"? Where, then, is Scripture's teaching on the purpose, purity, and pleasantness of the use of one's sexual desires and expressions?

The ultimate failure of using allegory to interpret this book of the Bible is the fact that the source of meaning comes from the interpreter's imagination and not the Scripture text itself. The usual signals in the text that this book should be taken as allegorical are missing. Thus, as it all too often occurs in allegorical interpretation, the text becomes whatever the interpreter wants it to be. Furthermore, no two allegorists agree on the meanings that each other assigns to these Scriptures, so there is a wide disparity in interpretations of what most texts in this book mean. As a result, allegory does not illuminate the meaning of the text; instead, it tends to obscure it!

For example, the early church father Origen, who mainly introduced and championed the allegorical method, used it with regard to Israel's exodus from Egypt. One of the midwives whom Pharaoh had ordered to kill all Hebrew infants was named "Puah," which Origen assures us means "modest," or "blushing." Since the color of blushing is red, her name stands for the shed blood of Christ, which of course was red. Unfortunately, instead of Origen helping us get closer to Christ, he takes us further away from the text, so that in the end the text has nothing to do with its meaning. It was not until the Protestant Reformation that many of the reformers in general abandoned the allegorical interpretation. The efforts to resolve the tensions many saw between the text's literal sense and what was thought to be normative in other parts of Scripture were deemed a failure.

But if allegory is not the key to interpreting this book, what is? To be sure, there are only 117 verses in the whole book of the Song of Solomon, which comprises 470 Hebrew words, 47 of which appear exclusively in this book. The Shulammite maiden speaks 55 of the verses, with a possible additional 19 verses added to her total.

The book is attributed to Solomon in the very first verse of the book,[1] and he is mentioned later on as its author. This "song" was apparently one of 1,005 songs he wrote (1 Kings 4:32, though the LXX says he composed a total of 5,000)! This song is called the very best song by using the expression "Song of songs" since Hebrew does not have a superlative form, but uses the repeated noun in a possessive mode (cf. "King of kings" and "Holy of holies").

WHO WAS THE SHULAMMITE MAIDEN?

The Shulammite was a young country maiden from the village of Shulam, located in the territory of the tribe of Issachar, where she lived with her mother and brothers. They assigned to her the care of the grapevines and nut trees that seem to have been somewhere near her village. She had a boyfriend, who was a shepherd, one to whom she hoped to be married to or engaged to be married to one day in the future. Not much else is known about her except her physical charm, which will be treated in the commentary that follows.

---

1   "The Song of Songs that is [or, belongs] to Solomon" (my literal translation of the Hebrew).

THE CHARACTERS IN THE BOOK

In addition to the Shulammite maiden, there are the following characters: a shepherd-boyfriend who is totally enamored with her; King Solomon, who also finds this maiden very attractive; the brothers of the Shulammite; the ladies of the harem of Solomon back in his palace; the women and citizens of Jerusalem; and a choir who occasionally joins in with their song about her. The final remarks in this poem are made by either Solomon or a sage.

PLACE IN THE SACRED CANON OF SCRIPTURE

A famous quotation in the Jewish *Mishnah* counters any questions about the canonical status of the Song of Solomon:

> All the Holy Scriptures render the hands unclean.[2] The Song of Songs and Ecclesiastes render the hands unclean. R. Judah says: "The Song of Songs renders the hands unclean, but about Ecclesiastes there is dissension." R. Jose says, "Ecclesiastes does not render the hands unclean, and about the Song of Songs there is dissension." . . . R. Simeon ben Azzai said: "I have

---

2 Soiling the hands is used to describe those books that are considered to be canonical Holy Scriptures.

heard a tradition from the seventy-two elders [the Sanhedrin] on the day they made R. Eleazar ben Azariah head of the college, that the Song of Songs and Ecclesiastes both render the hands unclean." R. Akiba said: "God forbid that it should be otherwise! No man in Israel ever disputed about the Song of Songs to suggest that it does not render the hands unclean, for all the ages are not worth the day on which the Song of Songs was given to Israel; for all the Writings[3] are holy, but the Song of Songs is the Holy of Holies."[4]

The canonicity of the Song of Songs was accepted by many of the church fathers. For example, Hippolytus in the third century expounded Song of Solomon 3:1–4 at Easter. However, Theodore of Mopsuestia (d. 429) incorrectly declared that neither Jews nor Christians should ever read the Song in public. Moreover, the reading of the Song was assigned to the eighth day of the Passover celebration, which Jews and Christians together celebrated by reading the Song of Solomon up to the time of Constantine.

---

3 The Writings are known in Hebrew as Kethubim, the third section of the Old Testament.

4 Herbert Danby, *The Mishnah: Translated from the Hebrew with Introduction and Brief Introductory Notes* (Peabody, MA: Hendrickson, 2012), 782: *m. Yadayim* 3.5. More famous is the statement by R. Akiba in *t. Sanh.* 12.10, where he denied access to the world to come for any who sing the Song of Songs at a party or in some profane way.

THE INTERPRETATION OF THE SONG

Few books have suffered as many extremes in interpretation as the Song of Songs. This is why most of us can empathize with the annotations made to this book by the seventeenth-century men of the Westminster Assembly:

> It is not unknown to the learned what obscurity and darknesse of this book hath ever been accounted, and what great variety of Interpreters and Interpretations have endeavoured to clear it, but with so ill successes many times, that they have rather increased, than removed the cloud.[5]

Some have treated the Song as a sort of outline for the history of Israel from the exodus to the messianic age. Nicholas de Lyra argued for the fact that the book described the progress of the church under the old and new covenants. Theodore of Mopsuestia thought it was Solomon's response to complaints that he had married Pharaoh's daughter. Martin Luther saw the book as referring to Solomon's political relations with his subjects. In the Middle Ages, some identified the Shulammite maiden with the Virgin Mary, and Jewish interpreters linked the Shulammite with

---

5   *Annotations upon All the Books of the Old and New Testament*, 2nd ed. (London: John Leggat, 1651).

the "active intellect" that humans strove to be united with. Others viewed the book as a poem expressing Solomon's love for wisdom just as Proverbs 8–9 affirmed such love of that monarch.

MY CASE FOR REVIVING AN OLDER THREE-PERSON INTERPRETATION

The literature and commentaries on the Song of Solomon are extensive. For example, Marvin Pope of the Yale Divinity School wrote in 1977 a commentary for the Anchor Bible Series, in which he included a fifty-five-page bibliography on the Song of Solomon that had more than one thousand entries. But even his list, which was selective, had no entries beyond 1975 and missed some notable contributions!

Those who have taken the more recent traditional allegorical and typical approaches to the book have assumed that the purpose of the Song is to teach something of the relationship between God and his people, whether that be in terms of the history of Israel or in Christian terms of Christ and the church or the soul and the Virgin Mary.

But there is an older three-character view that sees two male protagonists in the Song. These interpreters (similar to my approach) typically argue that the purpose of the Song is to teach the value of true, faithful, monogamous love in contrast to gross polygamy with all its degrading features that occurred in Solomon's court as the years went by. It disapproves of scheming, wantonness, ostentatiousness, and licentiousness. What is approved of, on the other hand, are simplicity, beauty, purity, virginity, and faithfulness. In that sense, then, the Song may indeed have been written as a critique on the Solomonic court—his wicked lifestyle and attitude. Yes, he loved the Shulammite girl, and he lost her. But God still instructed him to record his loss in order to warn all who followed in his steps. Here is how Calvin Seerveld puts it:

> The Song, with Solomon as a miserable case in point, not as a villain, was given to teach the sex-saturated populace who had forgotten the Way . . . of the Lord, the meaning of faithfulness again and to capture the hearts of frustrated men and women by the telling of the beauty, joy, and freshness of human love that honored the Law of the Lord. When the fear of the Lord ruled their man-woman love relationships again, [however], the fact that . . . [Yahweh] was a jealous lover of Israel would not be so foreign to their consciousness.[6]

E. J. Young of Westminster Seminary in Philadelphia comments similarly:

---

6   Calvin Seerveld, *The Greatest Song: In Critique of Solomon* (Palos Heights, IL: Trinity Pennyasheet Press, 1967), 76.

The Song does celebrate the dignity and purity of human love. . . . The Song, therefore, is didactic and moral in its purpose. . . . It reminds us, in particularly beautiful fashion, how pure and noble true love is. This, however, does not exhaust the purpose of the book. Not only does it speak of the purity of human love; but . . . by its very presence in the canon (for, in the last analysis, it is God who has put these books in the canon, not man), it reminds us that God, who has placed love in the human heart, is himself pure. . . . We are not warranted in saying that the book is a type of Christ. That does not appear to be exegetically tenable. But the book does turn one's eyes to Christ. . . . The eye of faith, as it beholds this picture of exalted human love, will be reminded of the one Love that is above all earthly and human affections—even the love of the Son of God for lost humanity.[7]

Though the Song is explicitly erotic, it does not give the slightest hint of crassness or of a fertility ritual or cult that was so prevalent in the ancient Near East. Instead, the Hebrew wedding marriage ceremony was called *kiddushin,* meaning "the consecration," wherein the couple "consecrated" themselves to each other in a promise of mutual sharing.

---

7   Edward J. Young, *An Introduction to the Old Testament* (Grand Rapids: Eerdmans, 1960), 354–55.

Nor are the references to human sexuality intended to cause embarrassment or shame. Instead, sexuality in marriage is a gift from God that is to be enjoyed, as the rare biblical allegory in Proverbs 5:15–21 demonstrates. The theme of the enjoyment of one's sexuality and its consummation runs throughout the whole Song and is central to the relationship. Notice that the woman is not reticent to take the initiative in the relationship, for almost twice as many verses come from her lips than from the man's. She is quite open about her longing for love and her willingness to give herself freely to her boyfriend.

This commentary attempts to revive a view of this Song that two centuries or so ago was the dominant view— one that sees two male protagonists: King Solomon and the shepherd-boyfriend back home. Solomon, for all his wisdom, fails miserably to understand how strong and abiding is the commitment of love between a man and a woman whom God has brought together. Solomon thinks he can easily woo this girl with the promise of riches, perfumes, and the opulence of the palace. But this woman places very little, if any, value on those things, especially in comparison to the gift of marital love that comes from God. Here, then, is the point and the reason for including this Song in Holy Scripture. The gift of love and affection for a mate of God's choosing is his choice gift.

So enjoy this teaching from our Lord to the blessing and joy of all young hearts who long to follow his will!

Chapter 1

GOD'S GIFT OF ROMANTIC LOVE

(1:1–2:17)

he Song of Solomon is not a modern novel, nor is it a poem of love; instead, it is the word of God proclaiming the beauty and purity of the marital experience in his master plan. Marriage comes as one of the gifts from our Creator's hands to us mortals—we who are made in his image. The idea of one man and one woman being joined together in matrimony and in a covenant with each other, as well as simultaneously in covenant with God (Prov. 2:17; Mal. 2:14), is central to this teaching. It is one of the great foundational teachings of Scripture. God presented it at the very beginning of his revelation in Scripture:

> The man said, "This is now bone of my bones and flesh of my flesh; she shall be called 'woman,' for she

was taken out of man." That is why a man leaves his father and mother and is united to his wife, and they become one flesh. (Gen. 2:23–24)

In its brief 117 verses and 470 words, Song of Solomon tells us how deeply moved and how greatly impressed Solomon was by the unshakeable love of the Shulammite maiden for her absent shepherd-boyfriend. Despite all the gifts Solomon could offer to her, including adding her to his growing harem as one of his new wives, she steadfastly refused him in favor of her shepherd-boyfriend to whom she was engaged. And she was a mere country lassie who also tended sheep on the hillsides. So this is a book with three main characters and not just two actors (a popular interpretation of this Song in recent years): King Solomon, the Shulammite maiden, and the shepherd-boyfriend back home. More will be said on this matter later in the book.

It should not be such a remarkable concept that God would devote a whole book of the Bible to this single theme of marital love and the joy and blessing that accompanies it. God intended from the very beginning that this Shulammite maiden and her shepherd-boyfriend should be blessed with a marital bond that exists between a man and a woman, when they came together in wedded matrimony. In fact, the late Meredith Kline summarized the whole point of the Song of Solomon in this way: "What the incarnate Word did for the sanctity of marriage by his presence at the Cana wedding [John 2], so the written Word does by dwelling with joy upon [the prospect] of conjugal love in the Song of Solomon."[8]

In a similar manner, Sierd Woudstra commented: "[The Song of Songs] is the Word of God teaching us the beauty and purity of genuine love, one of the gifts of the Creator to his creatures. This love the Holy Spirit saw fit to picture in terms of mutual desire for fellowship on the part of those devoted to each other."[9]

Richard Hess makes a more recent assessment. Even though he does not adopt the view set forth here, he shares many of the same values:

> The Song is unique in the Bible, but that does not mean it has no place here. . . . It further enables the reader to appreciate that, while the prophets condemned sex in the service of the worship of gods and goddesses and equated such behavior with adultery, this is not the whole story. The Song fills a necessary vacuum in the Scriptures because it endorses sex and celebrates it beyond all expectation. Although abuse is possible

8   Meredith Kline, "Bible Book of the Month: Song of Songs," *Christianity Today,* April 27, 1959, 39.

9   Sierd Woudstra, "Song of Solomon," in *The Wycliffe Bible Commentary,* ed. Charles F. Pfeiffer and Everett F. Harrison (Chicago: Moody Press, 1962), 604.

and to be avoided, sex is not inherently evil, nor is it limited to a procreative function. Instead, sex enables an experience of love whose intensity has no parallel in this cosmos and serves as a signpost to the greater love that lies beyond it.[10]

Here is an objection that many believers will likely raise: Can God's people be wedded lovers and yet still walk in the holiness he expects of them? Or must sweethearts married to one another accept each other's love at the expense of their full spirituality and genuine love for God? But if that is incorrect, then why must I think that these are opposing realities? Is there not a balanced answer that allows for both a sweet and beautiful life of wedded bliss and a simultaneous love and the joy of walking in the light of God's word and in fellowship with him? After all, sex is God's special gift to mortals, not the devil's gift! So why is there such hesitancy to discuss it or embarrassment over its presence?

Was it not God who announced, "It is not good for the man to be alone" (Gen. 2:18)? This, of course, states the general principle that applies to most cases. But this does not mean that God cannot and has not also given the gift of celibacy and made similar benefits possible for those who love him in their singleness.

---

10 Richard S. Hess, *Song of Songs* (Grand Rapids: Baker, 2005), 35.

Since the single life is not God's plan in the majority of cases, should not our lives as mortals generally make more sense when we love and act in community with another living being of the opposite gender? God provided this relationship with another mortal in order to help us be more fulfilled as we live and work together in harmony as a couple fully dedicated to each other and to the Lord. Thus, God's remedy for Adam's loneliness was Eve, not a relationship with any of the animals or with another of the same gender! You can tell the difference between Adam's appreciation for the animals and his love for the newly created Eve, for as we have already noticed, when Adam saw this woman, he jubilantly announced, almost going bananas: "This is now [at last] bone of my bones and flesh of my flesh; she shall be called 'woman,' for she was taken out of man" (Gen. 2:23).

But how shall we interpret a book like the Song of Songs? Since it is so enigmatic, and since it has had so many different interpretations, who is to say which view is the proper way to interpret the Song of Solomon?[11] And the only answer, of course, is that we must defer to the human

---

11 Marvin Pope, *Song of Songs*, Anchor Bible Series (Garden City, NY: Doubleday, 1977), devoted 140 pages to the issue of interpretation, saying he was giving only a brief sketch on this subject (see p. 89). See also H. H. Rowley, "The Interpretation of the Song of Songs," in *The Servant of the Lord and Other Essays*, 2nd ed. (London: Blackwell, 1965), 337–63.

writer, who in olden times is the one who stood in the council of God and first heard these words. His meaning is the only meaning that is authoritative and reflects the point of view of heaven. But how do we get at that meaning? Doesn't everyone have their own interpretation of what this book means?

To get more details for this answer, we must go to the writer of this book himself, for he is the one who stood in the council of God and heard him speak. If we jump to the end of the story in this case to see what Solomon, the author of this book, concludes, we hear him say the following:

> Place me like a seal over your heart,
> like a seal on your arm;
> for love is as strong as death,
> Its jealousy unyielding as the grave,
> It burns like blazing fire,
> `like a flame of Yah[weh].
> Many waters cannot quench love;
> rivers cannot wash it away.
> If one were to give
> all the wealth of his house for love,
> it would be utterly scorned. (8:6–7, my translation)

So what does all of the preceding text mean? The answer is this: Solomon had tried unsuccessfully to woo this rustic country girl from an as yet unidentified little town of Shunem/Shulam[12] in Israel to be another one of his wives, but she remained loyal, as she should have, to her shepherd-boyfriend back home, to whom she was already engaged. Hence, as part of their vows to each other, the shepherd wanted the Shulammite maiden to have him in possession of her heart, so that it would be sealed against all other loves and male suitors. Even though she might be active in doing any number of things to show her love for her bridegroom, she would be sealed and closed off from all other activities that would compromise, hurt, or disappoint her beloved boyfriend.

The measure of the shepherd's love for the Shulammite maiden had such strength that he apparently would have died for her. For there is a natural jealousy that wants to protect, guard, and save love; this love burned deeply in his heart.

But this is not a natural "flame" (v. 6). This flame had come from the Lord himself! The Hebrew has the abbreviated form of *Yah* for the longer form of *Yahweh*. Most modern translators attempt to make this abbreviation

---

12 Cf. 1 Kings 1:3: "Abishag the Shunammite," who ministered to David in his old age and lack of heat, and the one some have thought was the same woman from Shunem known in Song of Songs as the Shulammite. Second Kings 4:8 and 12, as a matter of fact, do refer to a town named "Shunem," but the woman whom Solomon tried to woo was called a "Shulammite," a Hebrew form in which scholars suspect that the consonant "l" was an interchange for the consonant "n" (an interchange of two "liquid" consonants).

for the divine name of Yahweh into an intensifying adverb, "*mighty* flame," but there is no Hebrew lexical evidence for translating God's name this way.

As Solomon writes, he too sees that this love between a man and his intended wife is not something that can easily be swayed by gifts of gold, silver, furs, jewelry, or the like. You cannot wash away true marital love; even a river cannot carry such love away in its currents. Solomon had tried with all his wealth to woo and impress this girl, but all of that wealth was "utterly despised"; it could not be exchanged for the depth and joy of the "flame from *Yah[weh]*" and the gift of marriage to the right person, who was meant for the other partner. Such an intense desire for each other was nothing short of a flame from the Lord himself!

The author of this book is said to be Solomon (1:1). Not only is his name placed first in the book, but also his noted reputation as a close observer of nature is verified (as it is in elsewhere, e.g., 1 Kings 4:30–33). In Song of Songs 8:11 we learn that he planted vineyards, gardens, and parks (cf. Eccl. 2:4–6). This Song names eighteen plants and thirteen animals. The writer also shows a wide knowledge of products from the East. The book alludes to jewelry, works of art, and goods obtained from commerce. Solomon already had a number of women in his royal harem (Song 6:8), contrary to the clear warning of Deuteronomy

17:14–20. But he deliberately violated this warning (see 1 Kings 11:1–8). So this book was written sometime during Solomon's reign from 971 to 931 BC.

Some worry whether this book, with such low views of marriage on the part of the monarch, should be in the canon of those books that were authoritatively given by our Lord. But Jesus himself bore witness to the fact that it should be included. He referred to the entire thirty-nine books we presently call the Old Testament that were in the hands of the Jewish population of his day (which amazingly also included the Song of Solomon). Moreover, he said these were the books that were authoritative (John 5:39; Luke 24:27, 44).

It is true that the Song of Solomon is never quoted in the New Testament, but some commentators see allusions to it. For example, the reference to the "garden" as the place where God's blessing might be found recalls the "Garden of God," or "Eden," theme that runs through much of Scripture and is found once again in Revelation 21–22.

The literary shape of the book appears to have a somewhat dramatic form, but it never was intended for dramatization. Such practices, as far as we are aware, were unknown among the Jewish people.

The poem in this book presents a continuous story, contrary to what most current interpreters maintain, even though there is no strict chronological order that structures the Song. Its structure can best be seen in its use of repetitions, refrains, assonances, alterations, and other literary devices. For example, see the repetitions in 2:6 and 8:3; 2:17a and 4:6a; 2:17b and 8:14; 1:15 and 4:1a. There is also the fourfold adjuration of the court ladies (2:7; 3:5; 5:8; 8:4). The same inquiry occurs three times (3:6; 6:10; 8:5), and the Shulammite makes three avowals (2:16; 6:3; 7:10). The book is composed of monologues and dialogues, soliloquies and reminiscences, and dreams. The imagery of the Song is filled with country life and is full of vitality and charming similes. To sum up, the song is a melody of beautiful poetry that ranks extremely high among the works of lyrical poetry.

There are seven speakers or groups of speakers: (1) Solomon, (2) the Shulammite maiden, (3) her brothers, (4) her shepherd-lover, (5) his companions, (6) the daughters of Jerusalem, and (7) some inhabitants of Jerusalem.[13]

The way to determine a change of speaker is to note the change in the Hebrew text from the masculine to the feminine form of the pronoun. This distinction may be inferred from some translations that add intertextual notes on the change of speaker as headers in the margins of the biblical text (but not all agree or follow the lead of the Hebrew text).

---

13 There may also be an eighth speaker in 7:1–5.

A quick outline of the story in this book includes the following. In the small village of Shunem a virtuous maiden lived with her two, or perhaps even more, brothers, and apparently her widowed mother (her father is not mentioned, so he might have been deceased). Her duty was to shepherd the family's flock while also caring for their vineyards and a nut orchard. In the course of carrying out her duties one day, she met a shepherd at noon while they both were resting their flocks under the shade of a certain tree. This tree, then, became their trysting place, where mutual vows of fidelity appear to have been exchanged on that occasion, or at a later time when they once again met at the very same spot.

One spring day, as she was visiting her family's nut orchard, quite unexpectedly came King Solomon's palanquin borne on the shoulders of his retinue. When he observed this maiden, he was immediately struck by her unusual beauty and he determined to make her another member of his burgeoning harem. He had her brought to Jerusalem and handed over to the care of the palace women as he promised the maiden all sorts of gifts. But her resolve was unshaken, even by this king with all his proffered splendor and wealth. She only wanted to be reunited with her boyfriend back home. Solomon eventually came to realize how utterly useless his attempted advances were as this girl's virtue and constancy were unshaken. These virtues and the resolve that came with it finally made him yield in order to let her return home to her lover. The story ends with the lovers finally being reunited, and Solomon realizing that love cannot be bought or talked into, but is a gift from Yahweh on high.

Studying this little-known book promises to be fruitful, especially since the concept of marriage is now under enormous attack, redefinition, and all sorts of distortions. Instead of viewing marriage as a gift from God, all too many people unfortunately see it today as another possession or conquest to be seized—and with anyone or any gender they please!

LOVE'S DESIRE FOR AN ABSENT LOVER
(1:1–4)

The title of this song begins with a note about its superlative character. "Song of Songs" is the way the Hebrews characterized this story because it was the "best of the best." There just was no better song anywhere; it was God's song of marital love fulfilled in a marriage. This song was number one on God's hit parade of the equivalents of the CDs and DVDs in Solomon's day.

The opening scene takes place somewhere in Solomon's royal court where this rustic rural damsel suddenly finds herself among the unaccustomed splendors and accouterments of that court. Actually, 6:11–12 explains how it was that she got to the palace in the first place. It seems to have happened this way: one day Solomon's entourage passed by the orchard where she was working when Solomon suddenly spied her in all her natural beauty working in the orchard under the hot sun. She was summarily hustled off to Solomon's palace as a possible bride for the king, but for all the elaborate magnificence of the royal setting, the maiden's thoughts were still occupied with her beloved boyfriend back home. She muses in a soliloquy on the memory of his kisses and his love, rather than on all the elaborate fuss Solomon is now making over her. She does not give her boyfriend's name, but for her there is only one "him." His love is "more delightful than wine" (1:2b), a grape beverage (Hebrew *yayin*) that was distinguished from "strong drink" (Hebrew *shekar*), which had more alcohol in it.

Previous to this, she had lived a sheltered life in her single-parent home. It was here that her brothers forced her to do work equal to a man's in the orchard as well as being a shepherdess, which consumed long hours. But now, despite all the perfumed odors that fill the king's apartments, it all has no comparison to the fragrance of her shepherd-boyfriend's presence (v. 3) and the rustic setting in nature he and his lifestyle represent. Solomon can keep his royal

Chanel No. 5; she prefers the presence of her shepherd-boyfriend. Nature has a more appealing waft of smells than those Solomon sprays on himself or about his palace.

Solomon continues his enchanting ways, but the maiden's heart is still fixed on being drawn away only by her shepherd. She does not wish to be rude to the king, but his blandishments are not working on her (v. 4). It is thrilling, perhaps for the moment, to be pursued by the wealthiest king of the whole countryside, but real love is still the best love!

LOVE'S FEELING OF UNWORTHINESS
(1:5–7)

There is a clear difference between this girl from Shunem and the daughters of Jerusalem. She informs these society ladies about how different she feels compared to them (vv. 5–6). The Shulammite is deeply suntanned from tending the flocks and working in the nut orchard and the vineyards assigned to her; in fact, she is as "black" or "swarthy" as the "tents of Kedar."[14]

Not only is the Shulammite richly suntanned, but she is also "comely/lovely" (v. 5a), meaning in Hebrew a beauty that is more than superficial or skin-deep. She is pleasant to be with, and she has a beauty that is apparent in the home

---

14 The Kedarites were a nomadic tribe from northwest Arabia (descendants of the second son of Ishmael, Hagar's son), whose tents were made of goat and camel hair and were very dark in color.

as well. This causes the society ladies of Jerusalem to look with disdain on her, but she urges them not to stare at her in such a manner (v. 6a). It was the sons of her mother's (perhaps) deceased husband that had forced her to care for the vineyards so that her suntan is the natural result of working out of doors (v. 6c–d). The upshot of all this work is that she has not had any time to take care of her own person (= "my own vineyard," v. 6d), unlike the richly painted and perfumed ladies of the Jerusalem court.

Once more the maiden's thoughts about her boyfriend resume (v. 7). She wishes someone would tell her where her shepherd-lover is.[15] At about this time her shepherd-boyfriend and his flock would be taking time to rest at noon. Must she now wander among all the resting flocks to locate her lover by herself? Where can he be?

LOVE'S COMPARISONS (1:8–17)

Verse 8 comes from the ladies of the court of Jerusalem, who say in a somewhat sarcastic tone, Why don't you go and try to find out for yourself where your lover is? Why ask us? From their point of view, this will nicely and discreetly eliminate a possible rival who has just arrived in the court—unwelcomed, of course, from their perspective! So hurry, they say in effect,

---

15 Apparently verse 7 was what she said aloud or as a soliloquy.

for it is the custom in our country for unmarried women to pasture the flocks and to water them, isn't it?

Solomon addresses the Shulammite as "my darling" (v. 9; Hebrew *rayah*, which occurs nine times in the Song, spoken by both Solomon and the shepherd). Solomon uses it here and once more in 6:4, but her boyfriend also uses the word seven times of her (1:15; 2:2, 10, 13; 4:1, 7; 5:2).

The king likens the Shulammite to a "mare" hitched to one of Pharaoh's chariots (1:9). However, one would never introduce mares into battle among all those stallions, unless one wanted to create pandemonium among the male studs, for the male horses would be distracted by the mares and forget all about the battle. Modern women would not take such comparison to a mare pulling one of Solomon's chariots as a compliment, but among Orientals such a reference to a steed was a great compliment. Solomon, of course, had several chariot cities, including Megiddo, Gezer, and Hazor. So the king promises all sorts of costly gifts in return for the maiden's love, but she will have none of his horsing around! The Shulammite prefers her shepherd-boyfriend!

Solomon goes on to compare the Shulammite's beauty to that of his magnificent horses, which have every hair of their manes and tails brushed to a glowing luster, and wear bridles of gold, silver, and costly gems. The king will add even more jewels to the Shulammite's already glowing cheeks so that her neck will be lined with "strings [and] chains of gold" (v. 10b) along with earrings to match. In verse 11 the king associates the palace ladies with himself as they together will replace the common bead necklaces worn by this country girl with costly jewelry.

While the maiden and the king are seated at his table (v. 12), she recalls the words of her "beloved" (a title used twenty-five times by the Shulammite and seven times by others). But his girl cannot enjoy the feast set before her at the king's table, for her inner turmoil continues to build as she recalls her boyfriend's words: "How beautiful you are, my darling! Oh, how beautiful! Your eyes are [like the eyes of] doves" (v. 15). His is a love that keeps on giving, and he recognizes her love, not for what she can do or give, but for who she is. She in turn compares her lover to a bundle of myrrh twigs that hang at her bosom, which continues to give off a beautiful aroma (v. 13). These two are deeply in love with each other, to say the least!

Even the fragrant cedar beams in the palace, as beautiful as they are (v. 17), are not enough to change her mind about the priority of her love to the one to whom she has pledged herself. She knows that the palace is not her place. A shepherd's tent with a grass floor and surrounding hills will do well enough for her because she will be with the one she loves—and that is what matters!

LOVE'S VIRTUES (2:1-7)

The Virtue of Modesty (2:1)

Because of some interpreters and hymn writers, who attributed 2:1 to Christ, it has become somewhat of a tradition to see the praise mentioned here as belonging to Jesus (as in the hymn: "He's the Lily of the Valley, the bright and Morning Star"). However, it is the Shulammite who speaks to the shepherd, and she compares herself to a simple wild flower with all the beauties of nature about her. The Sharon Plain, which bordered the Mediterranean Sea, was famous for its wild flowers and pastures. The "rose" here is a bulbous narcissus, and the "lily" (v. 2) is most certainly the scarlet red anemone, which can be seen all over the Holy Land (cf. Matt. 6:28)—not the rose we think of in the West. The shepherd, on the other hand, sees her as beyond a match to all other girls he knows (2:2). She is like one of those scarlet anemones set among "thorns." That is how she stands out! She is one beautiful woman!

The Virtue of Exclusiveness (2:2-3)

The Shulammite, in turn, compares her beloved (v. 3) to an "apple tree" (a citron tree), for he too stands tall and straight, strong and able to produce the effects of his work like a delicious fruit tree. That is how he stands out from all the other young men (v. 3b). Then she recalls the "banqueting house" (v. 4), or house of wine, to which she and her boyfriend have walked in the past. That banqueting hall was more like a vine arbor near a wine press, where they had shared a lunch together. What she has seen at Solomon's palace is a huge spread canopy with a banner inscribed over it to welcome his guests to the banquet. Nevertheless, the shepherd has something she cherishes much more than the elaborate field canopy especially prepared outdoors for a royal banquet: it is the delight of the shepherd's presence that covers her as a bower of love as it arches over both of them in loving devotion to their joint love for each other.

The Virtue of Desire (2:4–6)

This bride to be married to the shepherd-boyfriend is in a very delicate position: she is now separated from her beloved shepherd and is in the palace of the king of her country. This is why her love for the shepherd makes her feel depressed. While "raisins" and "apples" (v. 5), or "citrons," will satisfy her appetite and make her body healthy, they are no substitutes for her beloved shepherd. "Hope deferred makes the heart sick" (Prov. 13:12), so her desire is that grapes dried and pressed into cakes will have sustaining qualities and eating apples, or citrons, will revive her by their taste and odor. Nevertheless, she still wishes and longs for her lover to be present to uphold and protect her as his right hand embraces her (2:6).

The Virtue of Purity (2:7)

Therefore, the maiden adjures the ladies of the court at Jerusalem not to attempt to awaken or to prematurely kindle love by any improper or unfair means (v. 7). She has already given her heart to the shepherd, so all attempts to flatter her into switching her allegiance to Solomon, even though he is the king of the land, will be unjust and an unfair stirring of love before it is time for such a consummation of their love. She wishes to be left alone, just as the "gazelles/roes" and the "does" of the field show the same kind of shyness, but who are also quick to leap to an escape. She is as content as she can be!

LOVE'S ANTICIPATIONS (2:8–17)

Suddenly the Shulammite hears the shepherd's call come echoing across the valley. She has heard his distinctive call summon the sheep of his herd so frequently that she knows who it is that gives that call. It is him! Perhaps this all happens in a dream as it takes her back to the recent past when at her rural home in northern Galilee she had imagined that she saw her lover bounding over the mountains "like a gazelle or a young stag" to her bedroom window (v. 9a). What physical agility and what athletic prowess he possesses. "There he stands, behind our wall" (v. 9b), in his playful gestures, still calling her away to a new life with him. That is him alright!

In verse 10 the shepherd calls for his girlfriend as he puts the feelings of his heart into words. He now tells her why she ought to come with him. "See," he exclaims, "the winter is past; the rains are over and gone" (v. 11). This may also be a metaphorical reference to the time of their separation as imaged in the metaphor of the "winter." He has waited for her for what seems to be too long. But since the rains are over and gone, the paths and the roads will now be passable just as the streams and creeks have returned to their normal state and her foot will not slip now that things are drying out a bit. In fact, the wild flowers are out in profusion and it is now a time for singing (v. 12). Even the fig tree has begun to grow; at the end of winter it had green and delicate little buds, but then they filled with juice and now they have turned red in the spring, just like their love is now beginning to bud and stir from the dormancy of its "wintertime" (v. 13).

In 1:15 the shepherd compares her eyes to those of a dove, a reference no doubt alluding to their loving quality, but now he is calling her, as if she were a dove hiding or building a nest in the "cleft of the rock" (2:14), to no longer refuse his invitation and to join him in the fields. He really wants to see her. She (or more realistically her brothers), however, uses a vinedresser's ditty as an excuse for her not dropping everything to leave her work and go to be with him (v. 15). There is work to do, either her brothers or she protest, since the vines are in blossom and they have to be protected since they are vulnerable to the little foxes that will do their destructive work if she does not prevent them. That is why it is impossible for her to come right at this time. Both the young foxes and jackals often wreaked havoc with Palestinian vineyards as they played among the vines, dug holes near the vines, and ruined fences. They were mainly carnivorous, but they were also fond of young grape shoots and the grapes. The vines had to be protected.

If verse 15 is the speech of the brothers denying the maiden's freedom to marry, as we may suppose, her response is in verses 16–17. "You may indeed keep us apart in this way, but you cannot change the reality that the shepherd and I belong together. We will be joined together at some time." Then she addresses the shepherd in verse 17: "When the day begins to cool off and the shadows begin to lengthen at the close of the day, you come as speedily as a gazelle or a young deer bounds over the hills of Bether." This must be a poetical allusion to the obstacles raised by her brothers, for the Hebrew word *bether* means "separation" or "division," even though this is the name of an actual site near Beth-abara (2 Sam. 2:29; or Bithron) that was separated from the rest of Israel by the Jordan River and cut off by hills and valleys. "So do come soon, shepherd boy."

CONCLUSIONS

1. Romantic love is a gift from God. It involves deep longings, shyness, modesty, and feelings of unworthiness, yet the joy of a beautiful companion is a blessing from the Lord.

2. Position or power is no substitute for real love in a mate, which comes as a gift from God. Solomon records, under the inspiration of God, how he loved but lost this girl to a boyfriend back home. All his wealth, position, and power meant little to this beautiful girl in comparison to the gift of God's love for her man, the shepherd in her life.

3. One may give a whole palace full of gifts of gold, silver, and jewels, but doing so cannot quench true marital love, for that love is as a "flame of Yahweh." It is unequalled and not like anything else!

4. Times of separation during the engagement period can only make real love stronger rather than seeing it weakened by greater offers from other suitors.

5. "My beloved is mine and I am his" (2:16) is one of the sweetest and most enduring of all the associations given to us in our earthly journeys. Our marriages are heaven-sent gifts to lighten some of life's loads along the way. As the Jewish proverb says, "In marriage you share the troubles so that they are half as bad and you share the joys so they are twice as good."

STUDY QUESTIONS AND DISCUSSION STARTERS

1. Given today's values, do you think a beautiful woman in our day would turn down a romantic offer from a king?

2. I had a philosophy teacher who defined love this way: "love is an emotional response to an intellectual evaluation of another person's character, physique, gifts, and the way they present themselves in private and in public." What do you think about this definition? How would you define romantic love?

3. Are physical expressions of love to be reserved for the time of one's marriage, or are there appropriate physical gestures that can be gradually introduced in courtship as a couple grows more serious in their intentions to marry?

4. Is the interpretation given in this commentary appropriate for including the Song of Solomon in the Bible? If you prefer another interpretation, which one would you suggest as more fitting?

5. Why do you think God included a physical aspect to our emotional makeup? Would it not be too risky given the fact that we are made in the image of God?

Chapter 2

GOD'S GIFT
OF INTIMATE
MARITAL LOVE

(3:1–5:8)

o the anguished dismay of our loving Creator, our Western culture (if not the global culture) has swiftly moved to accepting (or at least tolerating) same-sex marriages, cross dressing, and sex changes, along with many other deviant forms of human sexuality. Even the word "homosexuality" has been dropped from normal conversation in favor of "lesbian, gay, bisexual, and transgender/transsexual" (LGBT). To this original group of letters, this powerful coalition has now added the letters QIA, referring to "queer/questioning" (Q) "intersex individuals" (I) and those whose bodies were born gender "ambiguous," along with other "asexual persons" (A). So now it's LGBTQIA.

The LGBTQIA coalition is united in its conviction that human beings were not graciously created male and female—at least in any significant or important way by God. Forget about your body, they say, for the important factor is the heart, where your will and especially your desire reside, and this desire can only be known by each individual person's expression of that will anyway. Some in this group, claiming a Christian basis for their actions, grab Galatians 3:28 ("in Christ there is neither male nor female") as their proof-text from the Bible, which is a misunderstanding of what Paul intended in that Scripture. They are willing to use any argument to validate their easy denial of their bodies as made in the image of God in favor of their physical sensations and physical desires.

The created gift of showing proper regard for one's body (either maleness or femaleness) gives way to fulfilling one's own wishes, desires, and will. Such super-imposing emphases on their personal passions, they say, must be done apart from any normative reference to the bodies they inhabit—or the gender they happen to possess!

Biblically informed Christians, however, rise up in strong protest against such a distortion. They affirm that the gift of God given to each person is the uniqueness of her or his body, even while their protest is accompanied by a simultaneous loving regard for the persons involved in this distortion apart from their practices. Our bodies do matter, for they are choice gifts from a wise and loving Creator. Our Lord made these bodies of ours, both male and female, and set such high value on these bodies that he made them in his own "image and likeness," and then pronounced them "very good." Moreover, our Lord asserted that "it was not good that a man should be alone" (Gen. 2:18), for he made us to have the joy of a life-companion of the opposite gender to share the joys and sorrows of living together. Sexual distinctions are not to be viewed as some accidental spin-offs of an unguided and unplanned evolutionary process. Rather, they are to be regarded as purposefully endowed sexual gifts given by God for the joy and blessing of each couple.

But can such a biblical doctrine be preserved today, especially as U.S. courts (with courts in several other countries following suit) have moved to close the marriage debate altogether and unconstitutionally impose, from the judge's bench, legislation that legalizes a gay marriage along with other possible aberrations of the moral law? Short of a heaven-sent revival, it appears it may be too late to hope that a doctrine of religious liberty and freedom will save a nation, such as ours, from the social, moral, and physical consequences that such a redefinition of marriage would bring. To oppose the biblical norm of a defined commitment between one man and one woman in a covenant with each other, and in a covenant with God, has enormous consequences. The ominous silence of the American news media on the danger of the possible loss of the prerogative of religious liberty and freedom in this matter for Christians and others is both frightening and deafening, especially because that silence comes from an otherwise noisy press and social media. The political and popular clamor for same-sex marriages is so strong that all other values are being jettisoned in an attempt to be more "up to date" than those who cannot see this is the way for a society that is determined to destroy itself!

But how can such a distorted view of marriage happen right before our very eyes—especially when marriage has its origins in the decree from God himself as found in the Bible? The gay marriage lobby and its bed fellows need to take only one more step, that is, the linking of their quest for unfettered sex and marriage between any two persons of the same sex with the cause of civil rights. Given the linkage of these two issues (i.e., gay rights and civil rights), religious liberty and religious freedom can be expected to be one of the first casualties that will follow on the way to a total calamity. Such a happening may be just a matter of a short time from now.

Bible believers must act quickly to restore the strong teaching of the Bible on the beauty of human sexuality in the context of biblical marriages. The teaching of Scripture is that God made the human body "good." The Bible also teaches that maleness and femaleness must not be sacrificed to the all-controlling desires or wishes of the person who wants to be something other than what God has made her or him. Our stand against those who reject the fact that marriage is between one man and one woman in God's normative plan for couples, their families, and their societies must be reasserted with all the passion and power that the word of God affords us.

In the sections that follow in the Song of Solomon, four descriptions are given of the material physique and shape of the bodies of these two lovers: one about the shepherd-boyfriend and three about the Shulammite maiden. Their physical forms are celebrated here with joy and thanksgiving to the God who made them as they are. Instead of provoking embarrassment at the directness and plainness of such a discussion, the description of the bodies of the man and the woman is meant to be an opportunity for rejoicing in the gifts of the Creator, who has made all things good after the counsel of his will. Certainly, such a discussion must be carried out with delicateness and sensitivity, but it must not be left in a vacuum for the evil one to fill with his own distortions and perversions.

The four descriptions of the human physical forms are as follows:

- the woman's gift of a body (4:1–7)
- the man's gift of a body (5:10–16)
- the woman's gift of a body again (6:4–7)
- the woman's gift of a body yet again (7:2–8)

To be sure, there is a balanced sensitivity here as the Scriptures delicately raise what might initially be seen as pure sensuality in these texts, but there is nothing to suggest indelicate crassness, unspiritual crudity, or just plain carnality or pornography. Instead, the body is beautiful, lovely, and a gentle and most pleasing gift from God. The praise the couple offers for one another's physique is a true description of their God-given appreciation and praise to our Lord for the beauty and the excellence of our Lord's work. Therefore, the gift of their bodies plays a normative role in their being called together as a couple and partners in the grace of life.

It may be true that there are some expressions and references to parts of our bodies that we in our culture would consider indelicate and perhaps not proper for mixed company, but this would be because of our different cultural standards and background sensitivities. Moreover, these odes in praise of each other's physical excellences are actually praises to God, who made the human body in the first place. Thus, physical beauty and the pure desire that couples have for each other are directly ordained by God. In fact, we would sin against God if we were to choose to be mute in our admiration for each other, and thus we would thereby show that our senses had been dulled or distorted to the point that we would not express delight and praise for God's handiwork in the creating of the man and the woman and the world around us. So mark it down: the lovers' praise for each other is another one of the graces of life sent from God. They are cause for singing praise to our creative Lord and not a basis for self-indulgence or showing off as if we were the makers and shapers of our own bodies.

This, in fact, may be a problem for many husbands, for men are often too reticent, if not too stingy, in fully and regularly verbalizing their appreciation for their wives' beauty and the joy they have brought into their lives by the presence and obvious gifts they possess from the Lord. Instead of withholding praise, our Lord desires for couples to be generous in the praise they offer each other in the recognition of the gifts each has been given. So let us go to the Scriptures and see how this emphasis is taught.

THE LONGING FOR MARITAL LOVE (3:1–5)

The Shulammite gives an account to the court ladies in the palace of Jerusalem of a troubled dream she has had of losing her shepherd-lover. As she lays in the palace luxury on her soft, spacious bed, puffed with fleecy covers and pillows, her boyfriend is all alone out in the fields as he keeps watch over the sheep and goats by night (vv. 1–2). In fact, she uses (in Hebrew) the plural word "nights," so this must have been a recurring dream.

There is no doubt she longs for him, for four times she declares him to be the "one my heart loves" (vv. 1b, 2c, 3c, 4a). In her dreams she mentally searches for him, but at first she does "not find him" (v. 1c). So in desperation, whether in her dreams or in actual reality,[16] she "[gets] up" and goes searching for the one her heart loves (v. 2a, c).

She rises from her bed again, as she hastily dresses and sets out in the dark (or: was it only in her dream?) to search for her lover. At first this search yields nothing except the city watchmen, who are making their rounds inspecting the city as they suddenly cross paths. Her question to them, though a bit strange from the watchmen's

---

16 We cannot say for sure, though it makes more sense to say it was only in her dreams.

viewpoint, is: "Have you seen him whom my soul loves?" (v. 3). The love of her life is now one of her top priorities. She has to find him!

However, shortly after encountering the city's watchmen, she finds her shepherd-boyfriend (v. 4). Her search (or dream-quest) is successful. She holds him and will not let him go until she brings him to her mother's home, into the very room where she had been conceived (v. 4d–e). However, all acts of moral impropriety are excluded in this description. Her words seem to support the view that her father had long since died and that is why her brothers have taken over the responsibility for directing her and guarding her reputation and virginity.

TWO INTERLUDES (3:6–11; 4:1–7)

A new scene is presented in 3:6–11, perhaps as a flashback to the ongoing story. This section tells us how Solomon and the Shulammite came to meet each other: a royal procession of King Solomon, who had just arrived in Jerusalem from a trip to the countryside with a possible prospect for another wife in his harem. The circumstances and other parts of this story as to how she got involved in such a situation will be told in more detail later (6:11–12), but for now she suddenly finds herself in a new setting—in the palace of the king.

The narrative begins with a "cloud of dust," or a "column of smoke" (3:6), which rises as the leading herald of the approach of Solomon's palanquin/sedan kicks up a dust storm. However, despite his not being clearly visible for all the dust, his approach is nevertheless announced by the smell of perfumed odors that accompany his coming. Sixty mighty men, all armed and ready to protect the king, bear the platform of the royal palanquin on their shoulders on which is seated King Solomon on a royal throne (vv. 7–8). Surely, the stomping of 120 feet on the dusty road is enough to have raised a cloud of dust that precedes Solomon's arrival. Such was the impression that a king in that day could make as he arrived in all his pomp and circumstance.

If the story thus far has been properly reconstructed from the details of this text, the Shulammite maiden was already being considered for a part in the king's royal train. She nevertheless was still insignificant although she had by now, no doubt, been made a reluctant member of that royal procession. Solomon is specifically named in this passage three times (vv. 7, 9, 11), but the Shulammite does not merit a single mention at this point. This no doubt may have been the first public appearance that this maiden may have made at the royal court.

In the interlude in the text (3:6–11), Solomon's "carriage" (sedan throne/chair) (v. 9) is described. It is made of cedar wood from Lebanon. It has posts made of silver and its base is of gold (v. 10a–b). It also has a seat upholstered in purple. This sedan, or palanquin chair, apparently is a love-gift from the ladies of the king's entourage/harem, for it carries the inscription on the back of the rider's seat "[With love] from the daughters of Jerusalem" (v. 10d).

As the story continues, a second interlude in 4:1–7 appears, where the beauty of this maiden is further described. This section begins and ends with the words "How beautiful you are, my darling! Oh how beautiful" indeed (v. 1) and "All beautiful you are, my darling; there is no flaw in you" (v. 7). The description that follows is a strong detailed proof of the truthfulness of that double affirmation. These must have been words spoken by the shepherd-boyfriend as the palanquin of Solomon momentarily paused in its journey close to the grapevines and nut orchard in which she had been working. Her boyfriend realizes that the maiden is under enormous pressure to go with the king, yet despite all the pomp and regal displays of the king, his quiet words of love might be more than a match for all the glitter, excitement, and noise made by Solomon. This should help men in our day express their joy and happiness in God's special gift of a wife each husband has been given in the grace of God. "If it is felt, men, then it must be tell't" goes the saying! Love should never be taken for granted.

The shepherd-boyfriend goes on to mention the beauty of the Shulammite's eyes, as another quiet indication of his love. Even though he uses words he has used before (v. 1c), who cares if he repeats himself? Her long hair also reminds him of a scene he has seen many a time off in the distance: a flock of goats clustered together gracefully streaming down the hillside, making the same movement as the long soft strands of the Shulammite's hair as she tosses her head from side to side!

The shepherd continues his praise of the Shulammite by referring to her teeth. Many in that culture often had several teeth missing. But the Shulammite's teeth all are present and white like a flock of newly washed sheep (v. 2), perfectly shaped—each paired off with its neighbor and none out of place! She is the picture of beauty and she has a smile that goes with her mouth full of teeth!

Her lips are a natural red color, symbolizing good health (v. 3). The same is true for her temples (perhaps a reference to her cheeks), which are like a pomegranate when broken open and displaying its rosy hue of edible seeds. Her neck (v. 4) is long and tall, as distinguished-looking as a tower or a citadel of David, which was built of white marble and stately in form. In David's tower, the trophies of the king's victories were hung on the wall (Ezek. 27:10–11), and so it is that the maiden's graceful neck should also be adorned with an ornamental chain of pendants similar to what other Oriental women wore.

Among Orientals it was not considered immodest or unnatural to refer with admiration to a woman's breasts, for at the very least they symbolized the fact that a woman had reached the maturity of womanhood and was ready for the life of marriage and motherhood (4:5). At last the shepherd-boyfriend informs the Shulammite maiden that their separation is only temporary and that he will go back to his mountain site to wait for her (v. 6). Finally, he reminds her once again of his enduring love for her (v. 7).

THE PROSPECT OF MARITAL LOVE (4:8–11)

Those interpreting this Song with three main characters—as I am doing here—will find 4:8–11 to be their most difficult passage. The problem in this text is that the shepherd-boyfriend addresses his love as his "bride" and "sister." This has led many to assume that the young couple was at this point already married. But as we have stated earlier, the Song is not in a strict chronological order. The best way to understand these allusions to his "bride," therefore, is to take them as proleptic, that is, as a prospective view on the order of events, as the story races ahead for the moment to indicate how things will eventually end up.

In fact, the sudden use of "my bride" (v. 8), "my sister," and "my spouse" (vv. 9, 10, 11; 5:1) distinguishes this section from the others in the Song. But this does not indicate that the marriage has been consummated at this point, for after the shepherd has described the Shulammite's beauty, he now dwells on the graces of her character. He therefore boldly proclaims her to be his "bride"—that is, according to the proleptic view proposed here, his bride to be! And she renews her pledge in 4:16b, as they prepare for the coming marital bliss in 5:1. He longs to be alone with her (4:8), to be aroused by her (v. 9), to be attracted by her lovemaking (v. 10), and to be affected by her sweetness (v. 11). What a romance this is, but also what a picture of the joys God has intended for all marriages to experience in the grace of his covenant with the couple! How gracious of the Lord who has given marriage as a gift to mortals to teach us the delights, pleasures, and designed happiness that our Creator built into marriage as his special gift to men and women!

THE EXCLUSIVENESS OF MARITAL LOVE
(4:12–15)

The shepherd proceeds to describe his loved one, using the figure of a private garden. Solomon uses the figure of a "well," a "fountain," and "streams of water" in his allegory on marital fidelity in Proverbs 5:15–23, where he boldly makes a strong case for absolute faithfulness and exclusivity, and where he describes how this privilege is one that is very private and to be shared only between a married couple. It is not to be shared with any other person.

In the Song of Songs, the picture of a "garden" is used seven times (4:12, 15, 16; 5:1; 6:2, 11; 8:13). It is always presented as a picture of the maiden. She is a "locked garden" (4:12), which is bolted and secured from the inside of the door. This, then, indicates the maiden's virginity, for in the Arabic tongue, a "deflowered virgin" was an "opened" woman, one who no longer was a virgin. Thus the Shulammite is wholly and totally the shepherd's very own companion. Since water (the metaphor being used here for their marriage) was so scarce in the ancient Near East, Jewish gardens were often hedged about or walled up enclosures with self-contained fountains. Likewise, this couple was reserved for each other's private enjoyment. The man was expected to protect and hold back from public view his marital partner (cf. Prov. 5:15), for their love was to be reserved solely, exclusively, and unreservedly for each other and for no one else!

The "garden" is further described in 4:13–14, for the word "orchard" is also capable of being literally rendered by the Persian word "paradise," such as could be seen in the parks and pleasure gardens surrounding the palaces of Eastern monarchs (Eccl. 2:8). The trees are dark green with foliage and full of fruit, filled with tightly packed sections of seeds. This is perhaps a symbol of fruitfulness or pregnancies desired in the forthcoming marriage. A good supply of water comes from springs both inside and outside the garden (Song 4:15), but it is not to be wasted or left to run in the streets (Prov. 5:15–17)—a symbol of any form of adultery, prostitution, premarital sex, or so-called free love!

THE PRIVACY OF MARITAL
LOVE (4:16–5:1)

The possessiveness with which this couple holds each other can be seen in the liberal use of the pronouns: "my garden" (4:16; 5:1) and "his garden" (4:16; 6:2). The gentle breezes and the strong winds are needed to make the garden productive (4:16). In biblical times breezes helped fertilization by pollinating gardens as seeds were blown about, and winds strengthened the growth of the roots. In Israel, the enormous force of the north wind was broken by the Lebanon Mountain chain to the north, yet it was the north wind that also brought clearing of the atmosphere after a time of rain (Job 37:22; Prov. 25:23). The south wind, however, came in from the Arabian Desert and it brought hot, sweltering heat, but never stormy or rainy weather.

Yet its heat did help to ripen the fruit. Thus the shepherd desires that the Shulammite's charms might be appreciated by all who look on her and who see her just as he has come to know her abilities and characteristics. The last lines of 4:16 come from her as she invites her boyfriend exclusively to enjoy the luscious fruits of her loving care.

In 5:1 the shepherd gives his immediate and eager response to her invitation to come into her garden. In effect he says, "I will come, I will gather, I will eat, and I will drink." Note the eight times that the word "my" appears in 5:1. All of this is in response to her alluring invitation to "come into his garden" (4:16e). The words are playful and delicately put, but the sense of sharing the embrace of love is nevertheless temptingly present and part of their preparation for lovemaking.

THE JEALOUSY OF MARITAL LOVE (5:2–8)

With this paragraph, we begin the second half of the Song. We are back in the palace in Jerusalem as the Shulammite relates another dream to the court ladies in which she once again fears that she has lost her beloved boyfriend back home. This dream may have followed the one in 3:1–4, for she had remarked that she was having "dreams." Indeed, especially troubling dreams are bound to reoccur in such anxious states of mind. Here is another dream, but this one must have seemed more like a nightmare!

In the former dream (3:1–4) the maiden had gone on a search for her shepherd-lover, but this dream is initiated by her being aroused by the knocking of her shepherd on her door and his appeal to her to be given shelter (5:2). His call for her to "open to me" (v. 2c) is followed by four quick favorite possessive terms that he must have used as pet names for her.

He calls her "my sister" (v. 2c), which must have meant that back home in the village of Shunem, the two of them were regarded as if they were brother and sister. Even now, though they are apart for a time, and though they were once declared lovers, their friendship is still intact despite the separation forced on them by Solomon.

He also calls her "my darling" (v. 2c), a Hebrew word root that has to do with tending and caring for a flock. There is a yoke that they share and a tie that binds them together.

A third name he gives her is "my dove" (v. 5d), already used twice before in the Song, referring to her eyes. It is distinctive of mourning doves, however, that when they are alone or apart, they make a cooing sound to call for their mate. This is the relationship the couple also wants to enjoy.

Finally, he calls her "my flawless one", (v. 2d). This does not mean she is totally perfect, but it does mean that she stands apart from any defilement and that she is a complete person in her moral purity in his estimation and discernment.

All the hours the maiden has been sleeping, even with her obviously disturbing dreams, he has been outside calling for her, for the dew falls on his head and his hair grows wet from standing outside in the dampness of the passing night (v. 2e–f). But the maiden also feels she is in a quandary, for while she desires to be with her lover, her natural maiden modesty holds her back. Furthermore, she has already disrobed and washed her feet for the evening (v. 3), as was customary in Oriental style, so she does not want to get them dirty again now that she has retired to her bed. Nevertheless, in these few verses she refers seven times to him as "my lover/beloved" (vv. 2, 4, 5, 6 [twice], 8, 10).

The shepherd is seen in her dream in the act of reaching his hand through the latch-opening (v. 4) as her heart quickens and her emotions stir. In Eastern homes, there was a grill or a small opening in the door through which a caller might put his hand to beckon someone, or even to identify who he was. With this signal from his hand, she quickly dresses and goes to the door, stopping only to dip her hands into some perfume according to another Oriental custom (v. 5). The perfume is available because she must still be at the palace—a peasant girl might not have been able to afford such luxuries. Alas, however, by the time she gets to the door, he is gone (v. 6)! She looks for him, but he is not there. She calls for him, but he does not answer (v. 6d–e). But if this were a dream, as I have suggested above, it is not unusual for dreams to be filled with disappointments and all sorts of frustrations that tend to mirror some of life's frustrating setbacks.

Whether her lover was forced to quickly abandon his call to her because of the approach of the watchmen or some other type of interruption or disturbance cannot be determined from this text. But as she steps outside in her dream, she meets ill-treatment from the city's watchmen (v. 7). They take away her "mantle/cloak," which was a light wrap usually thrown over the head and shoulders when a wearer might hurry out-of-doors unexpectedly without thinking it might turn out to be a long time.

The following morning her first contacts are the palace ladies of the harem, who make up the "daughters of Jerusalem." She tells them her dream as she pleads with them: "O daughters of Jerusalem, I charge you—if you find my lover, . . . tell him that I am lovesick" (or "faint with love") (v. 8). This puzzles these women, for what kind of woman would turn down the affections of a fabulously rich king for some poor shepherd-boy back home? That woman would have to be crazy, or just plain out of her mind. What kind of love is this for some country bumpkin? Can it in any way trump Solomon's gifts and treasures? But she jealously holds firm in her affection for her country lover. She does not want the love of this monarch or any of his proffered gifts, no matter how wise or wealthy he is!

CONCLUSIONS

1. The love God gives to a couple is an ardor and a zeal that is so strong that kings and princes are not able to compete with it. The gift of real love exceeds all other gifts found in this world!

2. Marital love was intended by God to be exclusive, intimate, and enjoyable. Marriages without such a love must appeal to God for his gift to both of them, for without it marriage can be dull, boring, and just plain unenjoyable!

3. The power, strength, and characteristics of marital love come as a gift from God, which steals our hearts, delights our whole person, and supplies a rich fragrance to all of life.

4. Marital love is to be guarded and protected like a locked garden with its waters saved for refreshing one another, not to be shared with others.

STUDY QUESTIONS AND DISCUSSION STARTERS

1. Why is that so many in the contemporary culture are more interested in how they feel and how they can express their wills, emotions, and desires than they are in being appreciative of the gift of their bodies? How do you explain this? What effect does the teaching of the image of God have on such a discussion?

2. Why is marital love so exclusive? What can wreck that exclusivity? How does one protect that exclusivity and maintain it through all of life?

3. Why is marital love so jealous and private? Can that jealousy get out of hand? What are we to do in that case?

4. Should this Shulammite woman give up a life in the palace to be with a mere shepherd-boyfriend for the rest of her life? What would make someone turn down such a tempting offer? What does that tell us about the love God has given for couples who remain in covenantal commitment?

5. What is the balance between modesty and a proper gratefulness for the gift of our bodies? What do you think leads to the attraction of the body of a person of the same gender? What does Scripture teach about this?

Chapter 5

GOD'S GIFT OF
ABIDING LOVE
(5:9–8:14)

IN PRAISE OF THE SHEPHERD-
BOYFRIEND (5:9–6:2)

n 5:9 the women of the Jerusalem court wonder why the Shulammite maiden thinks her beloved is better than all other men, and even better than such a stately person as King Solomon. Our country lassie answers by describing the beauty of her country-lover in 5:10–16. The women of the royal court have been watching the Shulammite very carefully, and even though they have found her to be an exceptional woman of unusual beauty, who is as winsome in behavior as she is beautiful in appearance, they just cannot understand why she is still worried about her search for her rural boyfriend in contrast to the enormous possibilities of being a woman of distinction who might be a part of the royal harem of the most famous and wealthiest king anywhere! What is it about that shepherd-boy that makes him so special? Why would she even think of enlisting these court ladies in an attempt to locate him? What is the secret to his attractiveness and any alleged excellencies he might possess? That's what they want to know.

Everything about him is appealing to the Shulammite maiden, for she thinks him to be "altogether lovely" (v. 16b). She sees him as "radiant and ruddy" (v. 10a), the picture of health. His head is like the purest and finest of gold (v. 11a), while his hair is "wavy" and "black as a raven" (v. 11b–c). He too has eyes that are like doves, as he had claimed that she had (v. 12a), but his eyes seem to be mounted like jewels (v. 12d). His cheeks are to her like "beds of spice" (v. 13a), and his lips are like "lilies" (v. 13b) dripping with myrrh. Add to that his arms, which she sees as "rods of gold" (v. 14a) and his body as "like polished ivory" (v. 14c). His legs, she claims, are like "pillars of marble" (v. 15a). She goes on to speak of his appearance and his mouth in similar glowing terms (vv. 15c, 16a). So she speaks up and says in effect, "If you daughters of Jerusalem wish to know why I am so attracted to my lover, I hope that description will satisfy you!" As anyone can see, as far as she is concerned, her shepherd-boyfriend is just the tops!

It is important, isn't it, for lovers (and in this case we mean both the man and the woman) to tell each other those things that they admire in each other? Not only does it build up good will and strengthen the marriage, but it also is a great encourager to each other in building self-esteem, as well as building up the esteem found in each other, as the relationship is enjoyed in the marriage.

To get back to our story, the mystery of the whereabouts of the shepherd is solved, for the maiden now knows he is in his garden—"in the beds of spices" in the valley (6:2). Now, at last she can, perhaps, be reunited with him!

OUR MEMORY OF LOVE'S COURTSHIP
(6:3–8:4)

We now come to some of the most sustained teaching on what is involved in a godly, beautiful, and successful marriage.

The maiden begins in 6:3 with the affirmation "I am my lover's and my lover is mine." They are meant for each other in her view and all other intruders to the contrary must realize how exclusive their love for each other is. Their love will brook no rivals. They are meant to be exclusively for each other and for each other alone—and that is that!

These words are followed by the shepherd's praise for the Shulammite's beauty, which may have been spoken in the presence of the daughters of Jerusalem (vv. 4–9). Some argue that these lines should be attributed to King Solomon, as he makes one final attempt to woo this maiden into his harem, but the words seem to fit the shepherd's point of view much better. He must have composed these words as he traveled to Jerusalem, passing through the city of Tirzah (v. 4). Tirzah was described as one of the most beautiful spots in Israel, for it was for a brief period of time the capital of the seceding northern kingdom with its ten tribes forming the nation of Israel. Tirzah was located on a hill, some twenty miles from Shunem. When the capital of the northern ten tribes was later moved to Samaria, unfortunately Tirzah was forgotten about and tended to disappear from history.

It was during a conversation that the shepherd had with the maiden, just before she was taken away by King Solomon, that he spoke tenderly to her in verse 5. Her eyes have "overcome [him]" once more (v. 5a). He sees the love she has for him in those eyes of hers. Of course, the Shulammite is most distinct and set apart altogether from all the other sixty queens, eighty concubines, and virgins without number that Solomon had already acquired up to this time (v. 8), with an obvious disregard for what God had taught on marriage. No wonder 1 Kings 11:1–3 indicates that Solomon loved many foreign women, which would later soar in number to some seven hundred wives and three hundred concubines! His appetite for women showed no boundaries, such as those set by the teaching of God's word, and the boundaries that he himself had earlier expounded on as the word from God.[17]

As the shepherd praises the Shulammite in the presence of the ladies of the Jerusalem court, they begin to look at her in a new light. They suddenly realize that they have not really seen her as she truly is (6:10). She outshines all of them like the full moon glowing against a dark sky.

With this, the Shulammite begins to tell them who she is. Yes, she is just an ordinary girl in Israel, who makes no claim to fame or greatness. But her interest in the beauty of growing things in nature had taken her one day into a valley close to her home (vv. 11–12), into a garden where she and her brothers cultivated nut trees and where pomegranates were in bud and the grapevines had just begun to blossom. Her job was to tend to these plants and trees. She loved watching things grow in nature.

One day, however, she was suddenly surprised to see a sight perhaps she had never seen before. Her care

---

17 See once more the allegory on marital fidelity in Proverbs 5:15–23.

for the trees and the vines was suddenly interrupted by the magnificent appearance of Solomon's palanquin and sedan-chair, borne by sixty strong men carrying Solomon on his trip. This at first terrified her, as she ran as swiftly as Amminadab's chariots, or better rendered as the "chariots of my noble people." Whether this comment was made at that moment, or later as the story was related to them, the daughters of Jerusalem plead with this unusual maiden: "Come back, come back, O Shulammite" (v. 13a). They want her to return with them to Jerusalem and stay as part of Solomon's retinue/harem of wives. But why would these ladies, so used to all the messy and sophisticated intrigues in the royal court, want this country girl to join them when they knew what a pandemonium and awful turmoil that would raise? Was her beauty of such a sort that it added to the prestige of the whole court?

The text continues, and there are two interpretations of 7:1–5. One is that Solomon is here continuing his flattery in hopes of finally winning this maiden over to his side. The other interpretation is that this is the language of the women at the palace as they continue in their attempts to prepare the Shulammite for her further interview with the king about his forthcoming marriage to her. Whichever is the proper answer, the Shulammite is highly praised indeed. But it seems certain that verses 7–9 of this seventh chapter come from the king's mouth. Solomon reveals how struck he is by this girl's erect and stately posture, which is similar to that of a palm tree (v. 7). He is sentimental and refuses to give up his romantic blandishments, even when it is apparent he is losing in his attempt to win over this young lady—despite his regal standing, position, and power.

Finally the Shulammite speaks to her shepherd-lover in verse 11. No longer is she ambivalent about her paramour's love for her. She now calls him, "Come, my lover, let us go to the countryside; let us spend the night in the villages." All of this is to recall the memories of love's courtship back home and the invitations already given in 2:10 and 4:8.

Apparently, by this time the king has granted the maiden permission to return home if that is what she wishes. As she is released from the palace where she had been taken, she must have immediately sent the above message to her lover. Her interests now merge with those of her boyfriend, for she wants to get an early start on the trip back home from Jerusalem (7:12a). All the plants she had tended under the forcible insistence of her brothers are now in blossom. Even the "mandrakes" now send forth their fragrance as well (v. 13). The mandrake, usually regarded as a symbol of love, was often noted for its alleged aphrodisiac qualities. The presentation of the "mandrakes" here does not indicate an intention to prepare some type of magical potion to aid the romance (as if it were a kind of Viagra or the like), but it is only to match the maiden's state of mind, which is one of innocence and simplicity. The only reason for such an association between "mandrakes" and "love" seems to be that the Hebrew word for "mandrakes" is *dudim*, which some linguists link with one of the Hebrew words for "love," *dodim*. Maybe, but that looks like a long shot!

The memories, along with the sensations of love and the time of engagement, are here linked to the blooms that come in spring and the smells of new life, for this must be the playful association between "love" and "mandrakes." But the maiden also has saved up both "new" and "old" (v. 13) things for her love—such as fresh fruit from the spring crop and dried fruit from the past year's harvest. She has set these aside for her shepherd-boyfriend. This may be a metaphor for her claiming that she has reserved her virginal purity for him. Accordingly, their love will have been reserved for love's proper moment, fresh and creative, as well as familiar in some ways but always memorable and incomparably awesome.

So real and deep are the Shulammite's longings for her lover that if the shepherd were her younger brother, she would be more at liberty to express her affections for him with hugs and kisses without being charged with being too forward and lacking in proper reserved decorum (8:1–4).

This is why she yearns for greater closeness to him so that she will be able to do four things: (1) find him, (2) kiss him, (3) bring him home to her mother's house so he can instruct her, and (4) refresh him with something she has made with her own hands. She longs for the tender embrace of her shepherd-boyfriend (v. 3). All of this leads her to ask the daughters of Jerusalem once again: Why would they ever have wanted to stir up her presumed emotions of love for Solomon before she was ready for real love with her shepherd-boyfriend, and thereby rob her of the joy she was about to enter with her beloved? (v. 4).

OUR EXPERIENCE OF LOVE'S INVINCIBILITY (8:5–7)

In the view I am adopting here, there is no description of an actual wedding found in the Song of Songs. There are only the vows of love couples make to each other that usually lead to marriage. But now the final scene has been reached.

In a chorus, made up apparently of the villagers of Shunem with its country folk and neighbors, they together sing this inquiry: "Who is this coming up from the desert leaning on her lover?" (v. 5). The answer, of course, is the Shulammite maiden.

It all goes back to the "apple tree," or citron tree, where the shepherd had first awakened this girl's heart (v. 5c). It is not, therefore, a foolish sentiment to cherish and retain those memories of such secluded spots, where lovers have enjoyed sweet and private conversation. Such memories are to be stored up and brought to mind from time to time lest the freshness of marriage wears thin and becomes forgotten.

As we continue working through the text, we discover that marital love has five qualities: it is intimate, intense, indestructible, invaluable, and ineluctable.

First, such love is *intimate*. The maiden earnestly desires to be indelibly imprinted on her lover's heart. She refers to it as a "seal," which in that culture consisted of a small cylinder worn around the neck on a chain or on a beaded string of some sort as a form of personal identification. This identification seal could be rolled out on wet clay, or a ring could be pressed down on wet clay as equivalent to a personal signature. Both the seal and the ring were deeply engraved with characters or pictures that functioned as the identity or authorization of the person represented, much like a signature in our day on a check or an important document (cf. Gen. 38:18; 41:42; Jer. 22:24; Job 38:14; Esther 3:12; 8:8; Dan. 6:17; Hag. 2:23). Thus the seal was fully equated with the person himself or herself. No one else could carry that seal or identity. This, therefore, is a key sign as to how intimate and distinctive a couple's love for each other is.

True marital love such as this is also *intense,* for "love is as strong as death" (8:6b). This is not to say that such love manifests an immature possessiveness or that it insists on having its own way, but it nevertheless has an extremely deep bonding with such a strong intensity that there are few things that adequately compete with it. It wants to protect, guard, preserve, and give one's self to the other person. In fact, it has a "jealousy," or "zeal," that is as tenacious in its grip as the grave. That is how constant real love is—it defeats every attempt to suppress it or to overthrow it. Its intensity can hardly be measured! It is deathly strong!

A third quality of true marital love is that it is *indestructible* (v. 7a), for nothing can extinguish it. There is no amount of water, nor are there any rivers or floods that can wash away genuine love that God has placed in a marriage as defined in the Bible. This kind of love will persevere despite all the waves of adversity, suffering, or trials that can possibly arise in a marriage. Little, if anything, can destroy this love that God has given to a couple!

This type of marital love is also *invaluable* (v. 7b), for no amount of money or other types of gifts can ever purchase or divert this kind of love away from its object. Solomon with all the riches of his palace and empire had tried as hard as he could to attract the Shulammite's attention and favor. Nevertheless, even though he tried to win her and decisively lost, he was moved by inspiration of the Holy Spirit to record how he had loved this maiden, but eventually lost her to a lowly shepherd boy because he tried to substitute things in place of himself, whereas this couple only wanted to be exclusively with each other. Love will not tolerate the substitution of stuff, wealth, and riches as an alternative for the giving of one's self to another person. A love that tries to give all the stuff of this world in place of giving one's self is cheap and valueless and eventually harmful to a real marriage. It is not the love God gives as his gift; instead, it is an artificial substitute!

Finally, true marital love is *ineluctable* (v. 6e). The passionate call of this love cannot be evaded or escaped. Its flames are the very flames from Yahweh himself. This is the only place in the book where God's name appears. This love will blaze into full strength, but it is a flame that is not artificial—it is a "flame" from "Yahweh" (v. 6e–f). Since the flame is lit by God, there is little chance of it being extinguished unless that love is not tended and guarded with care!

To summarize, this love must be passionate, personal, persevering, persistent, and priceless. It is a special gift from God to all who recognize him as their Savior and Lord. Who said biblical marriages are not made in heaven? They were wrong! Such a marriage as described here surely is made in heaven!

OUR APPRECIATION OF LOVE'S GUARDIANS (8:8–14)

These final verses pose two options. They may indicate a time in the past when the Shulammite's family cared for her when she was very young and her family wanted to discipline and preserve her for the future. Or they depict the Shulammite's sister, or perhaps even one of the shepherd's sisters. Now that the Shulammite and the shepherd are married, she is a sister to both of them and needs special care to make sure she is kept as pure and chaste for her future husband as the Shulammite had been preserved for her shepherd during their courtship.

A "wall" (v. 10) serves as a good metaphor or symbol of stability and protection. Everyone watches over this girl to make sure she firmly resists all improper or immoral suggestions of potential suitors. If she, on the one hand, proves to have the attitude of a "door" (v. 9c), which here functions as a figure of speech for one who is too open and too accessible to the seductiveness of any who approach her, then her family will "enclose her with panels of cedar" (v. 9d). This means that her brothers will restrict her freedom for her own protection if she seems to be too easy going and too susceptible to all and any who might attempt to woo her.

But, on the other hand, if she is as solidly reliable as a "wall," then they will "build towers of silver on her" (v. 9b).

This must mean that she will have a worthy dowry given her when she marries if she acts properly during those days, as she comes into a time of maturing and seeking a spouse. The reward for the brothers' efforts, and the patience of this sister, is that this young lady will experience contentment and peace (v. 10d)—a type of joy that also comes only from the Lord.

Meanwhile, the contrast with Solomon's harem is enormous, to say the least, for he has a "vineyard in Baal Hamon" (v. 11a). The past-tense verb is used to explain this. His vineyard is called symbolically the "lord of a multitude," or the "lord of confusion." Thus, while the possession of a vineyard was usually a sign of opulence in agricultural terms, yet in Solomon's case, if this stands figuratively for his harem, it then is also a place of great turmoil and loud noisy murmuring among all these women with all their intrigues and infighting for position and favor in the royal court.

Solomon's "vineyard" (read: harem) strongly contrasts with the maiden's "vineyard" (meaning: her own person) in verse 12. Of course, her own "person" (read: vineyard) is of much humbler circumstance and without all the frills of the palace, However, she will now find pleasure in tending and cultivating the development of her own person (read: vineyard) and being all she can be in the interests of her beloved boyfriend. Yes, the second line of verse 11 literally reads: "The thousand be to you, O Solomon, and the two hundred to those getting fruit." This probably means: "You, Solomon, are welcome to your retinue of wives, your entire harem, along with all your revenue, and the long list of your tenants, who work all your fields, but I am content with what I have in my shepherd-lover. I will share my 'vineyard' only with him."

In verse 13 the maiden is no longer in Jerusalem, but is now in the country where she feels she belongs and so earnestly wanted to return as soon as she could. There with her friends, she is also most content to live with her husband, that is, her shepherd-lover. We can almost hear a cheer go up for her courageous stand and for the joy she now experiences. She has found her lover!

The book ends with verse 14, giving us words that at first appear to be unrelated to what has just taken place. But this is not so. The maiden's appeal reflects the call in 2:17 to "Come away, my lover," for now this invitation comes with new energy and emphasis. Now she exalts with abandon, for as she recalls how she was invited previously to downgrade that anticipated joy for all the glitter and glamor of the court-life she had seen, the contrast to what she now sees is enormous. For it was an even greater delight to go with her real lover at the speed of a fleeing gazelle, or to get away with him at the speed of a young stag. The story ends with the newly wedded couple riding off into the sunset, experiencing the joy and happiness given by God for marriages that covenant fidelity with each other and covenant abiding trust in the Lord.

CONCLUSIONS

1. The marital love God gives to couples who trust him and who make him part of their covenant vows is a joyous and an abiding love.

2. Such love cannot be traded or exchanged for any other person or gift, for God will make that marriage like a round seal written over one's heart with its hold on the two of them continuing to be as strong as death, yet one with unbounded joy and happiness.

3. Marriage, as God's gift, is intimate, intense, indestructible, invaluable, ineluctable, invincible, and inextinguishable, as well as personal, possessive (in the good sense), persistent, priceless, and princely.

4. And to the unmarried, Solomon under inspiration of the Holy Spirit urges that they be a "wall," steadfast in their resolve to remain pure, and not to act as a "swinging door," too easily persuaded when they should not have been convinced at all.

STUDY QUESTIONS AND DISCUSSION STARTERS

1. In what sense are marriages between believers made in heaven? What tends to fracture such an arrangement?

2. How does this new couple take up the challenge of looking out for their younger sister? In what ways should we also show the same regard for those in our family or among our associates who are younger than us, but who are approaching the age of marriage?

3. What, out of all possible gifts, did this couple find to be the most basic one they sought through their marriage? How realistic do you think this choice is for us in our day? What would you say is highest on your list of priorities for your marriage (already or the one you transpose?)

4. What characteristics mentioned here are as true of this marriage as you think they are also true of your marriage or the way you aspire to behave? What action or attitudes have you seen in other marriages that you wish were not there and that are inhibiting full joy and blessing from God on those marriages?

5. How important is a good theology and doctrine of marriage to the stability of a nation? Will nations that take a lesser or more secular view of marriage risk

collapse of their economy, social fabric, influence, and military ventures? If so, why and what can be done to forestall such a tragic conclusion to such a culture?

Printed in the United States
by Baker & Taylor Publisher Services